Plainswoman:
Her First Hundred Years

Poems by
Kathleene West

Sandhills Press, Inc.
Ord, Nebraska

Published by Sandhills Press, Inc., 219 So. 19th St., Ord, NE 68862

Library of Congress Cataloging in Publication Data

West, Kathleene.
  Plainswoman: Her First Hundred Years
Vol. 1 of the Plains Poetry Series
first edition
Library of Congress Catalog Number: 85-50677
ISBN 0-911015-04-4
ISBN 0-911015-05-1 (pbk.)

Cover drawing is by Paul Otero, R.R. 1, Box 27, Chimayo, New Mexico 87522;
The illustration is based upon "Plain Talk from the Platte River."

The Plains Poetry Series is edited by Mark Sanders and J. V. Brummels.

FOR PAUL SCHACH

Acknowledgements

The author thanks the editors of the following publications in which poems from this book first appeared: *Cincinnati Review:* "Hired Girl"; *The Round Table:* "Land of Opportunity," "Ellis Island, National Park," "Bounden Duty"; and *Poetry Northwest:* "Grandmother's Garden." "Wind Chill" first appeared in *Prairie Schooner* copyright © 1984 by University of Nebraska Press. "Grandmother's Garden" was also published in *All My Grandmothers Could Sing* (Free Rein Press, 1984). "Over the Gravel and Through the Town," "Plain Talk from the Platte River," "Farm Wife," "The Garden Plot," "Flowers-de-Luce," "Terrae Filii," and "Grandmother's Garden" were included in Kathleene West's *The Garden Section* (Yellow Barn Press, 1982).

Thanks to the Fulbright Program and the Ministry of Culture and Education, Iceland, for grants to Iceland where some of these poems were written.

The Nebraska Arts Council, a state agency, has supported the publication of this book through its matching grants program funded by the Nebraska Legislature and the National Endowment for the Arts, a federal agency.

Contents

I

"I feel very strongly that I am under the influence of things or questions which were left incomplete and unanswered by my parents and grandparents and more distant ancestors. . . . It has always seemed to me that I had to answer questions which fate had posed to my forefathers, and which had not yet been answered, or as if I had to complete or perhaps continue, things which previous ages had left unfinished."

—C. G. Jung
Memories, Dreams and Reflections

The Muse Invocates

I sing through a woman and bless her
with my voice, with word and rhythm
I neither knew nor wished for.
As Calliope spoke no verse
but descended to the helm of the imagination
with courage and the shade of companionship
to the poets who paused before the chaos
that obscured them from the poem,
so I enter her and allow her to believe she knows me.

The only calliope I knew
came to town one summer,
and its steamy hoot made me jump
and reach for Luke's arm.
"We'll get married," he said,
and after came all my life with him,
then Karl, and a deathbed scene
when this woman's speech
was but a baby's babble.

Preacher craned his head over the bed.
"Do you have anything to say
before you go to meet your Maker?"
I had the strength to whisper back,
"God was good to me!"
and saw the disappointment on his face,
the sorrow ease from my son's wife
as she almost smiled
and I almost breathed.

Plain Talk from the Platte River

You out there, flanked by mountain ranges,
the foothills dark with soaring fir and cedar,
speak of *plains*
as if you'd lose your breath
scaling the clods turned up by the plow,
as if the creeks had to be kicked
into the rivers, sluggish with boredom under a massive sky
that extends a sameness over miles
and miles of homely soil.

Why should water rush
to get away?
After rain, the Platte's as blue
as Crescent Lake, lingers
as the sun lingers on each glossy leaf
of the willow, the Russian olive,
waits for creeks and the ghosts of creeks
to join its leisurely stretch to the Missouri.
Lost Creek, Disappearing Creek,
Bone, Thin, Dry Creek
name the gullies, the cuts in the earth
where water might settle,
make the latent stream welcome as the child
named before birth.

Birth is a flood, extending generations of seed—
the plains ripple with their growing!
Full-headed wheat, the soft stems of soybeans,
grandly-tasseled corn outgrowing its furrow,
and milo, its leaves mimicking the distant flight of birds.
Fields swell with color!
The alfalfa waves crest and break in a spray of purple,
spattering the pastures with mauve.
And always, there is Sunflower
to preside over harvest.
Not corn knife, nor crop duster,
neither nickel-a-dozen bounty nor government spray
will keep away Sunflower.
Constant as the sun,
it nods its bloom across the plains.

2

This undulant beauty can take away
your breath and fill your eyes with tears.
If you are one to weep for love
or because of love
your tears will hold in the shallow corners of your eyes
as water seeks its own level
as the river whittles its banks
as the first rain clings to the windowpane
before it drops
and flattens into the earth.

Land of Opportunity

The days passed too slowly for words.
The sea was our world, our language one and limited
as the serene conversations one holds after a burial.
We read again the letters from America.

> Here the buildings reach unto the heavens.
> Here you will make a name for yourself.
> Nothing you propose is impossible.

I thought to follow my father, keep house and name
as my mother taught me,
simple expectations, confounded
by this multi-level anarchy
that topples the god-given order of the sea
into this pandemonium of landing—
a gabble of commands,
howls and barks that subordinate us
to a herd of indistinguishable bodies.
Like heathen children who have never honored the Fourth Commandment
we shove onto barges that give us to this island.

There is no earth to kiss.
I had no desire to touch my lips
to the splintered planks at the dock
or the filthy tile of this parlor of babble
where people shout as if to the deaf or the dead.
How Lazarus must have cringed
from the circle of faces around him
after his blissful submersion into oblivion.

> Can-you-hear-me? Do-you-understand?

I cannot speak
but my hand is still firm
and gives my name in the sturdy strokes
of pen to paper. *Olava. Olava.*

This brittle face checks my eye-sight.
This thumping hand, my lungs.
And he with the book cries No! to my name—

Down the steep stairs I walk,
clutching the rustle of my skirts into stillness,
directing my feet, toe to heel, hush my step.

They have pronounced me free
from disease loathsome or contagious,
find me neither lame nor weak-hearted.
Had I the words,
I would not argue.
I was not brought up to question
                              openly.

Olivia. Olivia.
I push the new vowels to the front of my mouth
and search for my father.
A man with a moustache winks.
I pull my coat tighter about me.

How will Saint Olaf recognize me as one of his own?
There are no saints in America
and the pilgrimage leads far away from heaven.

Ellis Island, National Park

It is the incarceration of her imagination,
where the Count of Monte Cristo chalks his bitter days,
the aged hero of Chillon sighs from the ship
and Mary Stuart reveals her whitened hair,
an island that given the proper turrets and towers
could lock up the one who knows the eternal secret,
banish the offender to violent boredom.
This is imagination.
Her sentence reconstructs the chaos of solitude
but of formal prison, what does she know?

Her lover answered a midnight call
to bail his wife out of jail.
She waited up to hear his description
of prison clothes, the anecdotes of arrest.
A simple case of possession, easily dismissed
as her child-misery when her sister's husband proposed
a tour of the State Pen, her inability to respond
to an electrical chair with something more sensible than tears.
She recollects her father's account of the inmate
who hollered through the bars, "Hey Alfred!
                          How're things down at the Skeedee?"
shocking the faces of the Fellowship Group.

This group is fresh and wiggly,
eager pre-adolescents released from school
to spit over the side of the ferry
and pummel each other with fiesty affection.
They are not immigrants, but invaders
that rush from the boat and advance down the musty corridors
to fill the Great Hall with the confusion of decades past.
They live in a young country
and are happier than they know.

Their chatter overcomes her attempt to cast herself back,
to walk past the appropriate ghosts
with a guide conjured from the stillness of long-cherished desires.
The park ranger leads them down to a dusty dining hall
and she fills her notebook with his narration,
a catalog of private heroics,
the women who married strangers on the spot,
the hungry families staring at alien food,
consuming banana and peel in unquestioning acceptance.

6

She writes it down to make it true
and disappoints the schoolchildren
who hope she's a reporter.

The man behind her recalls his grandmother
falling to her knees in joy and gratitude.
She envies his memory,
shuts her eyes to visualize the kissing post
and the celebration of reunion,
the bits of joy that should survive
in these mouldering rooms.

It is not enough to survive.

She cannot wait to escape from this island
to steal with her own confusion
back to the familiar disorder of the streets
where she walks unguided,
secure in her ignorance of danger,
absolutely alone, and free.

Dumb Show

Beware, beware
With the evening air
Come voiceless spirits
To steal your wits
As they snip your tongue
As they leave you dumb.

With the threads of deception, I embroidered this tale
to watch my sister's skin turn pale
as I whispered the mute creatures
that hover over beds with sharp shears
to seize the tongue at the point of a yawn
and use our language as their own.

She savored her fright
until she saw my elaborate concern
each time she took a breath to speak
or raised up her spoon from her porridge.
Her laughter stopped, her chatter mumbled
behind a splayed hand.
And when she shrank from Mother's good-night kiss
to appeal to me, the one
who taught the tactics of the airy thieves,
that look held me fast
and I suffered my scolding
from our father, who stood, still
and contained as a man receiving a benediction,
his hands folded before him,
only his powerful voice chastizing my sin.

The American landscape unfolds before us,
a great plain, unbound by mountain or forest,
relaxed in its freedom to give not,
nor to receive.
I watch my companions open their mouths wide
to stretch their speech across the horizon
and accompany their words with undisciplined gestures
as if to claw comprehensible phrases in the air.
Like a cat batting at wool
twisting down from the spinning wheel
they try to catch an American voice.

How fine to speak! To understand!
What wonders lurk in those crowded sounds,
resources rich and plentiful as the land,
a history blessed with prosperity
and opportunities galore for the silver-tongued man.

Sweet words I knew,
when did I last speak
openly to the world?
With what pride
did I snap out another line
                This is how we wash the clothes
                        bake the bread
                        sweep the floor
to the staccato chant
that sped our reluctance through daily chores?
Or gasped out the Lord's Prayer
in a single-breath competition?

Language is wealth and dexterity
and we are but impoverished puppets
aping our thoughts with jerks and spasms,
our grins carved from ear to ear
to substitute for speech.
The muscles hold,
fearful to let escape
one syllable of our devalued tongue.

Maid Servant and Mistress

after a dialogue in *Instruction Book in the English Tongue*
Reykjavik, 1875

Maid Servant: I understand you want a servant maid.
I'm cheerful, oxen-strong and never tire.
You'll like to have your every whim obeyed.

Mistress: Now if you really want to be hired
(We don't say "mistress" or "maid" nowadays.)
You'll have to show me it's your heart's desire.

Maid Servant: I'll try to talk the American way.
Of course I need the work. I can't pretend
It's otherwise I'm Sunday best on a week day.

Mistress: Can you wash, iron and mend?
Mix bleach and soap and starch the lace?
Rinse, wring and dry before day's end?

Maid Servant: I should think I can do what you say.
You'll never see the linen scorched or streaked,
The French knots flattened or the crochet frayed.

Mistress: I see. And tell me what you know about cookery.
A fresh and fine-cut chop's no smart cook's test—
But when we're down to neckbones, can you please?

Maid Servant: Indeed you'll see I'll do my best.
With bones, we've broth; if bread, there's
graveyard stew—
Enough to stay the unexpected, hungry guest.

Mistress: And with the heavy work—can we depend on you?
Stack wood, carry water, turn a carpet
Like a flapjack, handle ax as well as broom?

Maid Servant: To be sure I can manage that. It's not
The fancy words that get the hard work done
But breath, stout wrists and stubborn heart.

Mistress: Can you follow my instructions?
Answer promptly when I call?
Pronounce your English nice and clean?

Maid Servant: As you hear, I answer each and all
                Your questions, and suppose I make some sense.
                My accent's rough, but my head is level.

Mistress: Well, I'll take you, with wages
            One dollar a week, more than any girl
            Is worth, I'd say. All elbows and no experience.

Maid Servant: Then may I start at once? To shrink and shirk
                Is far more trouble than it's worth.
                You'll see I understand the worth as well as work.

Hired Girl

The first English I learned— *knife, fork, spoon*—
I repeated as I circled the table and placed each utensil down.
From the sideboard, Mrs. Bond corrected my consonants,
lamented my vowels.
She retraced my path
to tap the handle of a cup more in line with the edge of the table,
or to slide her handkerchief through the tines of a fork
as if someone who thought in Norwegian
had dangerous notions about domestic duties,
would exchange the cut-glass pitcher
for drinking horns bubbling with mead,
impale the loaves on the point of a short-sword
or tear the fowl apart with her hands.

She believes she teaches perfection
and approves the crisp technique I adopt in her house,
an effortless motion with no variation in rhythm
as I flow from task to task,
not like a river that meanders, swirls or rushes
according to the obstacles and diversions of geography
but like coffee dispensed from an urn
in cup after measured cup of identical brew.

When I mastered the vocabulary
limited to this work
of prepare and arrange, repair and clean,
she considered my knowledge adequate
and cared no more for my speech.
I could rattle off each part of the cookstove,
recite the furnishings and figurines
that inconvenienced each room,
but my lists of syllables and accurate accents
could not convert the agitations
that cluttered my heart
when I confused the whistle of the evening train
with the foghorn's sad song
or when I polished the silver
and shifted my gaze beyond the perfect surface
to my blurred and miniaturized reflection.

I go about my chores with my face smooth and stern
even when the flatiron bumps over the heavy unnecessary knots
on the underside of the embroidered linens.

"Take equal care with the stitches unseen."
My mother, who found her pleasure
in the unnoticed beauty of any work,
the invisible touches that transform competence to art,
could have taught her daughters,
awkward with their fancy needles, a thing or two.
But it is not my place to identify the flaws
concealed beneath the cloth.
Only the hired girl knows they exist.

When the Sunday guests gather round the dinner-table
and bow their heads for grace
and their glances slide from the companion opposite,
over the place settings and down to their laps,
what paths do their thoughts take
between the "God we thank Thee for this food"
and the amen-reaching for the spoons?
Do they imagine angels in heaven
trumpeting to announce the celestial feast?
Do they recall that rich moment of delight
when they promised to keep their first secret?
Or do they wish,
helpless and unbelieving,
for a power beyond all possibility,
to ease the pain of some irrevocable loss?

"In Jesus' name" signals me to deliver them from hunger
and I bring them at once their Sunday meal
in an abundance of bowls and platters.
The guests speak.
They praise the well-carved roast, the uniform lightness
of the biscuits, the brevity of the morning's sermon.
I can understand every word they say.

II

"Marriage . . . is still the beginning of the home epic."
—George Eliot, *Middlemarch*

To Take to Wife

What was it that enthralled me?
His eyes, bluer than the cloaks the wise ones wore,
bluer than a lake, caught in the damaged meadows
with a wind rippling its surface
so one thinks of it as never being still.
When he slept, his eyelids dropped but half-way,
and as a garden snake
coiled luxuriously in the summer sun
glazes its membranous stare in equal intensity
at rest or alert, so he spent his nights,
and when I woke and turned to him,
I thought he feigned his dreams,
controlled each muscle twitch,
and let the riddled syllables escape with his breath.
Who hides a secret with gaping mouth and eyes?

Little have I to do with mystery folk.
Jesus is a man clad in white clothing
who makes a miracle from his myopic belief
in the equivalence of things.
A well-trod road, a glassy lake,
a man napping on a pallet, another dead in a tomb—
they're all the same to him.
And when he feels the need for chat,
he shakes his partner out of sleep,
temporary or eternal,
and speaks the necessary parables
to occupy his troop of eager scribes.

My bridegroom meets the soft fingers of my morning caress
not with sighs and stretches
as waking folk are wont to do,
expelling the last slow inhalation of darkness
and extending their limbs like children
imprinting angels on the snow,
but with a tension in his muscles,
a color quickening his face,
that in the rose and lemon tints of early light
seems more a shadow than a flush—
and were I not well versed in his habits
I would say he renewed his acquaintance
with the depths he visited each night.

17

Did he wish to slip away
like the chieftain's daughters in the old story
who vanished from their bed-closets
to dance by the moon-skinned sea,
shredding the precious leather of their shoes?
Could he have seen the maidens,
been allowed one glimpse of a legendary life,
he would have loved his own.

It is no mistake to marry a man who dreams,
who manages a clear perception of any vision,
but I mistook his desire for the achievement.
He sighs to have something to yearn after.
The months increase his misery, and mine.
I have become a vice for him to master,
a replacement for the waste in his design.

The Matter at Hand

What was *drunkard* to me but another word undefined,
unmentionable as *love* or *failure*,
words whispered behind cupped hands
when polite conversation lulls.
Once I envied that no man's land
between the borders of palm and lip
and longed for initiation in the technique
of the lowered voice, the eyebrow aloft in a protective arch
over nostrils agreeably flared
as gentlewomen recite the stations of woe
and visualize the image of desire or fate
that leads the hapless ones astray.

My half-brother used to say,
"Only one thing worse than being talked about—
and that's not being talked about."
Bless his heart, he kept away
from anything comparative. For better or for worse
never held his hurt in relative terms
as a farmer who feels the pitchfork tine
insert its crusted iron through leather sole to tender flesh
blames himself first
for being a man, and vulnerable,
for being this man, and doomed to the ill luck
that sets him on this farm, married to this woman
who bears him the son who chases the horse
that kicks the gate that topples the fork
that pushes its prong through this foot.

That wasn't Otto's way.
One night when Luke was rough
and I calmed myself to soothe the children
I heard the smooth, untroubled voice,
"You bet I know you can whup me.
But what do you think I'll be doing all the time?"

That wasn't my way—at least it hadn't been,
but when Luke hit me
and knocked me down—Oh God!
I could drop to the floor and writhe
to remember it,
the pain that hovered over my head
like the foul mockery of a halo forged by devils

for the sinner who screams half her agony in shame.
This is hell, and I that disgraced wretch
who orchestrates every whisper, each unheard word,
the conversation at noonday tables
into one common refrain:
I hear her husband beats her!

Shall I probe the wound?
Explore with tentative fingers
the faintly tinted skin, scarce a different hue,
to brush the swollen purple, greenish-yellow and push
to discover the exact source of shame?
Why should I feel more degraded
to receive the blows
than he to give them?
Why is the fear that neighbors will talk
worse than fearing he will hit me again?

"Don't ask," Otto said
when he gave me the money.
"You know I live by my wits,"
and I was at the end of mine.
Fifty dollars to sunder what the Word of God joined together,
but the work of the word is long undone
and I release my decision.
It is written, separated into letters,
inked and pressed to join
all the news that's fit to print.

Matrimony

Schooled in hard work and obedience,
I prepared to take my place in an ordered world,
to learn the responses in society's liturgy
as once I chanted the sequence of multiplication,
the predictable decades of kings and queens.
Every night I repeated the same prayer
and loved the permanence of holy days fixed,
red-stained and immovable on the calendar.
Although I saw my mother die
and braided chains of wild blooms for my father's second bride,
I believed in changeless unions, unsullied
by restless variation, bulwarks of immutable behavior.

My expectations were defined and regular
as the cross-stitch that hemmed my linen towels.
I rejoiced in that tidy embroidery
and it took the bright eyes of Freyja
to find the wrong side of my needlework.
I would loop my thread around the knots of women lingering
after church or fingering bolts of muslin in the dry goods store
to learn their gestures as they shook their heads
or folded their lips marvelously straight.
These women were good as the ground
with their strengths
and with their seasons.

And when I married I assumed *wife*
would correspond with my uniform skills,
that my stubborn talents
would pair with marriage,
two and two, beast and fowl
and all the creeping things of the earth
shut in with Noah,
who celebrated God's dry land with vintage wine from Ararat,
and fell, drunk-naked in his tent.

How we laugh at his anonymous wife
scolding her way over the rickety plank
to the ark. You see, it was all Noah's fault
                because he miscounted the shrews!
Dull-eyed creatures that blur
the very grass they scamper through
and should the holy spirit appear to them

21

in a wheel of intricate fire and design,
they could not distinguish eagle from lion,
ox from man.

Did I look too high
as if to catch a glimpse of God,
and gazing always upward, myself seem low?
And so reverse the question:
Sought he all too often
for something dim and servile below?

First is marriage a sacrament,
a finite rite,
but altarwise we set our backs
and marriage waits before us, another way to live.
My thoughts confuse—I said at first"
another way to love.

Farm Wife

A woman learns it's more than wind and sun
that makes her weatherworn.
She remembers the man who said,
"You can't memorize the clouds."
His words sing in her mind,
a refrain from the song of her mother tongue,
a refrain more useful than prayer.
Over the pint-sized grave
the American preacher thumbed the Book
of Common Prayer. How common,
how expected, this ritual:

> *hunger no more, neither thirst any more*
> *neither shall the sun light upon them*
> *neither any heat*

The sun beats down.
Clouds of dust and ash swirl, fill the trail behind
but she could wend her way back
even across the water.
Follow the sorrows, each conspicuous sacrifice,
connect them like dots:
abandoned hunks of furniture,
ancestors in heavy frames, a child's frail bones
blaze the trail with pain.

With each necessity forsaken, each small death,
she raises her voice not in grief,
but in praise of what she still protects—
the delicate china limbs of a figurine
caught, mid-whirl, in a dance
and deep in the trunk, beneath the flat layers
                    of calico and linsey woolsey
the ripples of a petticoat, white and foaming as the sea.
The dance and the occasion for lace are distant as the sea.

Into the sun they walk, farmer and wife
pacing off the section.
The grasses rustle like crinoline!
Their beards twist into her stockings, small irritants
that cling as she breaks from the solemn counting
and hikes up her skirt to run,
run across the field!

This is the beginning—not of her life—
but of all stories hence.
Never will she tell her granddaughter,
"When I was young and beautiful in a village by the sea. . ."

Bounden Duty

"He shall not search whether it be good or bad,
neither shall he change it"
                                        —*Leviticus*

The sun rises on the strict rows of corn,
casting shadows down the furrows
in lines exactly perpendicular with the horizon.
The wind nudges the plumb line of each stalk
into a temporary unalignment,
scraping the leaves against the forged blades of the cultivator,
guided in a path unswerving, east to west, west to east.

In the farmhouse, the woman aligns the plates
on a crisp tablecloth, its stiff starchiness a necessity
even for the bacon-splatters of breakfast.
"Aw Shuck," he will say, even as he approves
the stack of griddlecakes, centered on his plate,
each curve equidistant from the rim.

Gasping for breath after prodigious gulps of milk,
the children squirm in their assigned places,
perfecting their skill of aiming kicks
with expressions consumed by the neutrality of eating,
but the thrill of misbehavior overcomes them
and inappropriate giggles distort their mouths.
"Sit still! Behave yourselves!" and they do,
after a short pout at the rules and customs
they will enforce in their time.

The girl will marry, the boys will farm
and although they will acquaint themselves
with methods and devices as yet undreamed,
they will strive for the order
of vegetables sealed in identical jars,
haystacks with mitered corners
and children settled down.

There is uncertainty enough in any life,
but for those who choose the uneasy partnership
with land and weather, the year's success dependent
on their fortuitous interaction,
every seed is a poker chip
and each cloud disguises destruction and deceit.

Nothing regulates rain or wind
nor prescribes the sun
with its daily behavior free
from accusations of right and wrong.
What disasters they bring are natural,
met with the unvaried response, "It can't be helped,"
and the stiffness of the upper lip extends
to cramp spine and spirit
into a rigid conduct, dependable, unchanging
while the atmospheric libertines
encourage or deny the blowsy fertility of the fields.

On the Frontier of Tradition

There are women who could recall another country,
a few familiar places by the sea
where they and youth went about together,
sharing a brief intimacy
which they can never recover.
What pleasure to reminisce with that old friend,
to compare renditions of that casual association
with innocence.

When they inspect their daughters before church,
the damp odor of hair slicked into braids,
the unmistakable scent of childhood
carries the smell of salt-drenched sand
and they begin to speak, as to a former acquaintance,
in a dialect unfathomable to their American children
whose puzzled faces remind the mothers of their duty.

They do not tell the stories of flaxen-haired maidens
tending cottages in the woods, scouring troll-tracked floors
with thumbnails and tears while dearly-beloved brothers
stave off pitfuls of adders by strumming lutes with their toes
and the good and valiant heroes swim shoreless lakes
to slay and redeem as needed.

They hand down a penny
knotted in a tight corner of a handkerchief
and admonish the children not to scuff their shoes
and learn well the lesson for the day.

> And thou shalt teach the words which I command
> diligently unto thy children, and shalt talk of them
> when thou sittest in thine house, and when thou walkest
> by the way, and when thou liest down
> and when thou risest up.

This the children memorize.
And before Sunday School, the boys kneel down
to pitch pennies in the dust. And the girls
spread out their skirts for a shield.
And the preacher's son revenges his loss
with threats to inform on the victor
who must deliver his profit to the collection basket
for their little heathen bretheren across the seas.

After services, the men pace the shade of the trees
east of the church
and the women group in the mid-day sun
to speak of the past week
and mark how the children of others have grown.
Their measured conversation fulfills their task
to preserve and pass down a history of righteous behavior
as intricate as the ancient alliterative stanzas
composed after heroic campaigns.

The women separate and walk down the steps,
their straight backs a signal
to the men and children
that it is time to begin again
the dusty ride toward home.

III

Wa la, ahte ic minra handa geweald
and moste ane tid ute weorðan,
wesan ane winterstunde, þonne ic mid þys werode—
Ac licgað me ymbe irenbenda,
rideð racentan sal.

Could I lift my hands
and escape for one hour,
one winter hour, then I with this host—!
But iron-binding chains surround me,
ride me, the ropes of my bonds.

—*Genesis B*

First Blizzard, the Plains

For this we fight the good fight?
Enslaved, degraded
by a season of stiff and snowfouled meagerness,
we blunder through the daily chores,
clumsy and harsh in our swaddling skins,
bears on mangy chains, pining for sleep.

Sleep burrows in a snowdrift
far across the thickened fields, another captive
dulled by the hypnotic cold of each repeated day,
the cold that issues out its ugly uniforms
to hunch our shoulders, hobble our steps
house to pigshed, henhouse to barn,
as we apportion the trappings of survival:
a measure of grain, a hunk of bread,
straw, scented with the sweat of harvest, softer
and fresher than our blankets stacked in fat slabs.

But the chickens bury their beaks in matted feathers
and hold back their eggs from the chill nest.
Cows queue at the stack, their nervous tails
slowed by tangled chunks of snow to a sullen sway.
Even the hogs trudge to the trough—
everything stupefied by the effort of routine.

Only breath fights to escape
with a stab to the lungs, a desperate rush!
to impale itself on rough scarves—
our panting labor, the words we would say
held crystallized, transmogrified
until the fire we build releases all effort, all potential
as puddles of helpless water.

We wait to watch the water disappear,
people of the land, it is our duty
to find comfort in cycles
even as our words expire
and their emanations waver before us.

We plod our awkward bodies
down narrow furrows in the snow,
hold our tongues, protect what breath we can.

Will this snow shrink into broth
and thaw the fields into familiar earth?
We clap our mittens over the stove.
The bits of ice dance,
hiss and steam inspire one more breath.

Midcourse

"The part of a missle's flight between burnout and
re-entry, during which corrective maneuvers are made."

Just ahead of the Dakota storm
the woman turns south.
The wind turns with her, against her,
disguising the highway with ripples of snow,
gusting as if to push her insignificant car further
                                    into the landscape,
to whip its insolent color into a blur of International red.
Road and field are one plain, undulant with snow.
A skiver of snow drifts across the woman's shoulders.
The weather forces itself inside the car, inside her.
The wind whistles dry her mouth
and never before has her heart
been so cold.

A landbeat away,
Mount St. Helens plumes ash and smoke into the atmosphere
to mate with the easterly wind.
Oh ancient parents! This mythic coupling is no guarantee
against deformity. Your wretched offspring escapes the Cascades
and drops, miserable and heavy on the Plains.
Red snow bloodies the bodies of spring calves,
bloodies them and buries them
before the conscientious cows can turn
to tongue away the rusty afterbirth.
Red snow, lush as an undertaker's carpet,
thickens the road.
No weather spy divined this.
A mountain makes its own weather;
so does the heart.

How easily myth moves into the mind,
chokes and deforms only in the wish
to shape it with words.
Plainswoman knows without saying
this is the weather of the heart,
the brimming heart abandoned to winter
like a forgotten rain gauge,
freezing, cracking,
and now the blood regenerates,
marking her way.

33

"You'll be a castaway," a friend said,
"a castaway on a familiar shore,
an exile who knows the language."

When she stops at Bloomfield
she remembers to order coffee
before the meal.

The snow thins, turns ashen,
and the customers hush
each time the hearty voice from the Nebraska station
explains the red snow.

Wind Chill

If I whirl my passion into this wind,
it mocks back with whines and nasal moans.
Whatever I bury in the snow, it finds
and fetches like a malicious puppy,
returning my cries in mouthfuls of air
I gulp and swallow, my windpipe blocked
by this rush to the pit of my stomach.

Capricious ally!
Where were you last summer
when the children gathered at the windmill
and kept your vigil for hours?

Old Waverer, Old Wailer,
you guided our viking fathers across the seas,
inflating their greedy sails
with the promise of power.
Your promise. Your power.
How strong you are in this place.
No mountains to hinder your frenzy,
no sea to challenge your shout.
You enter us and we bow before you,
the commandment etched in our skin.
Thou shalt not talk back!
The rowdy voices of our ancestors
cry unto us from our blood.
What have we done?

We have traded the luxury of greed
for a mute stubborness,
uncoveted, secure, our perennial mark
like the scar on Karl's chin
from the stolid kick of a plowhorse
willful and contumacious as any Swede.
Two teeth he lost
but he urged on the horses, finished the round
before he came back to black out by the well.

The evening blackens the snow into thick gray.
My shoulders submit to the wind.
I need rocks; I need water,
an insubordinate tongue of rough land
to thrust its rebellion against the sea.

I would straddle those rocks to shout down
at the break and clamour beneath my feet.
Let the sea take the pain from my voice
and dash it into foam. Again, again,
the violent sea would batter the shore,
our anger, our anguish,
translated into vanishing spray.

As I felt the sea crash its weight beneath me,
I feel my blood assail my heart,
and I cry out!
but a gust of air shatters the accents of my language,
flattens the rhythm into a passive hum.

The wind suffers no competition. In this country
the wildest noise we carry within us.

Ultima Thule

I cringe under the weather,
its sneers and insults a crafted torment
devised by the stepmother, shrill in her encroachment,
who forces the blue-eyed innocent to seek her fortune
                              deep in the forest,
to seek her fortune and discover death.

Oh Stepmother, send me back to the forest!
Let me wind my way through evergreens,
each trunk a sturdy waist for me to embrace.
Let me climb to birch and thin willow
where signs of graze on the reindeer moss
                              beckon me home.

But my feet push through level after level of snow
unbroken by a single stand of trees.
And who would believe those skimpy hills
can stretch steep as a mountain
with every snowbound step?

Stepmother, you took my hand
and guided me down to the ship.
What turned my face away from the craggy shore?
                    the last island framed by mist?

I have known my fate
for a thousand years.
We have stories of the foolhardy men
who sailed through the ice at the end of the world
and gave up their bodies for one rude map.
Explore! Explore! their shouts lodge in the dark.
I search for their snowdrowned bones,
blue and bloated with ice.
When I find them, I will kiss their crystallized lips
and they will arise, my brothers, my husbands,
their first breath bearing the scent of my kitchen,
their hunger stilled with my fine white bread.

I am restless as their unsettled spirits.
Rescue and nurture do not satisfy them.
Jealous and industrious as gods, they encourage the snow
to fill in the path behind me,
leaving no clues for my discovery,
freezing my tears before they fall.

I trust someone will follow my footsteps
but I shall leave no task undone.
Stepmother and I turn back to the house.
The uncovered bones whistle with the wind.

Phantasmagoria

We kick the snow clotted at our ankles
and shudder the mirror as we slam the door.
Something more than wind slips by us
to press the windows, ripple the blinds.
Karl mutters. Drafty old house.

A woman leans over the milk pail.
The milk is blue and skim, the foam frozen into crystals;
the woman's skin translucent, thinner than winter air.
She motions toward the table,
turns back to the cookstove.
I should be relieved
that someone else prepares the meal
but I am not pleased
to see those who gather to devour it.

The apparitions congregate at my table,
nod stiffly to each other.
How they have missed solid wood beneath their elbows,
a woman handing them bowls haloed with steam.
I have rescued the spirits
but even in their deadly silence
they are too companionable,
close as Lutherans crowding
at the communion rail, compressing
to make one space more.
It is not for me.
I do not break bread with menfolk
but the shade of a woman assumes my proper place
and I have nowhere to belong.

The ancestors know the rituals to deliver me,
the once-living counterparts of these pale ghosts
who can only will their regret to a kindred soul.

     I charge you, spirits,
     with troubling my life.
     I summon you to leave this house.
     Close those vaporous eyes and return to your exile
     that hovers you forever over rough seas,
     that eternal pilgrimage from Old World to New.

Have I the power to sponsor your passage?
to steady your step to unyielding earth?
What makes you think you can earn a living?
You shall not enter.
Return.

Their heads incline in wavering assent.
One by one, they rise from my table,
bow courteously to me and vanish.
The ghost of myself steadies the ladle in the kettle,
looks sadly down at the simmering stew.
I have been rude, but how can I succor the unliving?
How can I nourish the lost?

Fruition

We have altered the harvest to save it—
rows of dull vegetables pressured beneath lids,
apples and pears dried into wrinkled caricatures,
the chokecherries I stripped from wild bushes
now stiff with sugar and paraffin-sealed.

A carcass hangs in the alleyway of the corncrib.
We will saw it apart on the kitchen table
and boil it to bits that fit in a jar.

Last summer, cleaning catfish, Karl chided:

You are too concerned with bones.

They knock against the cooker,
ready for me to fish them out,
dress them with onions and soft potatoes
and serve my family.

I have confused my task.

It is not enough to survive

but without the green of garden and field,
the optimistic warmth of the earth,
my assurance shivers, thin with winter,
needing more savor than neckbone of beef,
a bright sweetness I could not stir into rhubarb preserves.

The children, our saving grace,
group at the table, their clear faces
turned expectantly toward the stove.
Oscar, namesake of a royal Swede,
glum with the burden of the first-born,
Helga, pouting her baby frown, her pure belief in self
and Alfred Nicholas, elf-child,
my winter saint.
Karl shakes his head at the child's thick black hair,
the rowdy cheekbones disturbing
the proper squareness of a face.
Some Swede, he says.

He balks at school. Quick as a button with numbers,
he cannot convince the suspicious school mistress

41

that answers without explanation are enough,
that his arithmetic divides the seed wheat
and multiplies the yield into the hollow granary.

     I don't know how I know it.
     I just know.

The day I turned the team around
a mile down the road to town
because I'd left my pocketbook dangling on the bedpost
and went back home, unloaded the eggs and cream to sell,
and refused to start again
until the sun set and rose over my forgetting,
I could not explain my dependence on the old beliefs.
Like a miniature Karl, he stood, shaking his head,
but in his small smile I saw my hope.

Alfr, I would give you the gift of laughter,
but how can I give what is not my own?
We are sober folk, serious in our work
and this is a grim season.
Eat your supper, child.
I have prepared more than enough.

IV

"Ignorant, I took up my burden in the wilderness.
Wise with great wisdom, I shall lay it down upon flowers"
—Louise Bogan

Over the Gravel and Through the Town

Bordered by hedge, bounded by sidewalk,
Grandmother kneels on quiet ground.
A meadowlark trills from the power lines
And Grandfather taps downtown.

    Stronger souls fight the cruel geography,
    Straighten their backs to the stubborn wind.
    Another pair work out their time
    In modernized life on a new-fangled earth.

Tamping down violets, wild from the creek,
Grandmother kneels on quiet ground.
A mile away, crops fail or flourish
And Grandfather taps downtown.

    Children of grandchildren make the pilgrimage,
    Sigh for the old days they never shared.
    Sentiment flowers like hot-house carnations
    Forced into color for Anyone's Day.

When Grandfather taps downtown,
He waves at the men on wondrous machines.
And Grandmother transplants the final perennial,
Her last—but one—gift to the ground.

The Garden Plot

I will please the spirits of this place.

I will dig my fingers into the earth.

I will feel the dirt rim my fingertips
as it begins the total eclipse of my skin.

As my mother and her mother before
buried a spoon beneath the house
to charm the malevolent troll
I force my fingers deep
and the seeds descend
little saviours that wait for rain
to burst their sepulchres
and transfigure the plain.

We are here to grow.

I am on my knees
sprinkling the soil over the blank rows
crossing my palms on their promise.

Below
the spirits gather
rude and demanding as children
caressing, pressing the turnips
clinging to rhubarb's fingers
pink and pale.

I have gifts.

I fill the earth
with the garden's sweet offer
potato sprouts, frail tomatoes
the gentle bite of radish
and beetroot, its thickness, its flesh.

I whisper to the spirits.

It is not enough to survive.

The crisp aisles of lettuce
lead me down
to the candelabra of squash
the suppliant
succulent bean.

I bend low over the earth
and nuture as I praise
praise this vegetable paradise.

Ethereal carrot tops!

Ascending onion!

I bid you grow
grow and be beautiful.

Flowers-de-Luce

I

The garden quickens.

I beat down the weeds.

What was delicate, grows coarse and sturdy—
sweet corn, tough as saplings, fibrous parsnips,
asparagus, wooden in its veins.

All the vines are rowdy!

Leaves scrape and rasp.

Everything
looks like horseradish

II

As I rise,
the earth rises
                in one rough circle on my knee.

What implants that nervous twinkle in the stars?
What god? What plague?

Chicken Little, the sky is falling

and gorgeous in its descent,
this inspired shower of meteors,
a lifetime of wishes
that pushes me down
to witness
the glorious pyrotechnics of war,
the elaborate design of each false peace,
a millennia of new years bursting
in terrible celebration.

III

It is not enough to survive.

I need the spunky impermanence of flowers,
luminous zinnias, incandescent tiger lilies,
tulips and iris displayed in geometries of love and fiery color.

My thoughts flicker
                    on pansies
and bachelor's buttons on widow's weeds.

The phlox creeps toward the bouncing betts
and surprise lilies spring
                    behind the gladiolas.

I sip honeysuckle,
grow quiet as chrysanthemum
and watch the last iris wrinkle
and shrink its petals.

Even as they fall,
they are strong enough
to illuminate my journey,
garden to garden,
earth to earth.

Terrae Filii

The crops are not so fine this year.
The garden will feed us
and I sing over the flowers
but the wheat shrivels
and the wind rattles the corn like dry bones.

How Karl storms to see me
refresh my tangled greens
with pail after pail of water.
If the crops burn,
he'd have us all burn.

One evening I stole
to the edge of the cornfield
and cast up a piece of flint
but Karl followed. "No trolls in America!"
so I let be.

Who's to say what brings together
man and dreadful sun?
Preacher says, the children to come.
Karl snorts, and if not so rude,
I'd do the same.

We bought the farm.
Smooth and sleek as a fish,
it glittered in the winter sun,
all the gullies and ravines filled,
the hills leveled by snow.

How we ached for Spring!
And a raw pain scraped us
as the earth rearranged with every thaw,
took on the shape of windbroken mules
and plowhandles twisted like crippled hands.

Put a Swede and a Norwegian together
and they'll tear each other apart —
then build a kingdom from the scraps.
It's our will to toil under the sun.
We strive for something more than wind.

Troll talk, Karl says.
But I saw him shake his fist at the clouds.
"What god, what god do we seek to please!"

I could tell him, but he won't believe.
It is not enough to survive.

We are the spirits,
                    We demand.
sons and daughters of the earth.
                              We sacrifice.
Our sweat sticks to the earth,
salt of the earth,
ourselves given to ourselves.

Grandmother's Garden

As she loved harvest when the final ear hit the bangboard
as she loved the exquisite snip and tie of huck embroidery
as she loved her children quiet in Sunday best
as she loved all beauty and the reward of rest after work
    she loved her flowers.

And when he took a hacksaw
and cut wide swaths, like a scythe through grain,
slicing high the stems of tulip and iris
to make impossible even a salvaged bouquet,
she turned back to the house
and busied herself with some kitchen task
to wait for the child, who ran from the shattered blooms,
her small fists clenched on a few ripped petals,
her breath lost in the flattened bed of bouncing betts.

"Grandma, he's killing your flowers!"

And Grandmother winked,
                yes,
                    winked
as if to say:

I'm not angry
but don't let on to Grandpa.
If he saw I didn't mind
it'd hurt him more
than whatever hurt it gives to me.
Not that he regrets the farm,
but with nothing to resist him,
he misses the zest to fight.

You see a cruel act
but you'll play out your part
in dreams cut down, arranged for another's delight,
the dry whiff of long-pressed hopes.

The plants still live.
He knows they grip the earth tough and stubborn as weather
or himself.
You won't catch him
pushing up the mazes of their roots
or kicking destruction into their plucky stems.

52

Even this violence is a masque of harvest.
Dry your tears and remember.
Plant flowers, child,
plant flowers and tell this story.